Original title:
In My Heart's Garden

Author: Elias Marchant
ISBN HARDBACK: 978-9916-90-658-3
ISBN PAPERBACK: 978-9916-90-659-0

Sunbeams Through the Cherished Boughs

Sunlight dances on the leaves,
Whispers secrets of the breeze.
Nature's laughter fills the air,
Brighten paths that we once shared.

Golden rays through gentle shade,
Tracing dreams that will not fade.
Every glimmer, every hue,
Reminds me, dear, of me and you.

Seeds of Nostalgic Longing

In the soil of yesterday,
Memories like seeds, they lay.
Watered by the tears we've cried,
Blooming sweetly deep inside.

Each petal holds a story dear,
Woven paths of joy and fear.
Time will dance upon the dust,
In these moments, love is trust.

Mossy Footprints of Memory

Footprints fade on mossy trails,
Echoes whisper, soft details.
Each step taken, wide and strong,
In our hearts, they still belong.

Beneath the weight of all we knew,
Nature holds our love, so true.
In the silence, shadows play,
Guiding us along the way.

Dew-Kissed Promises

Morning brings a gentle glow,
Dewdrops dance, a soft tableau.
Each shimmer holds a vow unspoken,
In the dawn, our hearts are woken.

Promises like fragile glass,
Reflecting moments as they pass.
In the light, the world awakes,
Filling dreams with what it takes.

Childhood Dreams in the Thicket

In whispers of the breeze, I played,
A world where innocence stayed.
Among the trees, in sunlight's gleam,
I danced within my childhood dream.

With laughter echoing through the leaves,
Time spun gently, like spiderweaves.
Each secret path and hidden space,
Held memories I still embrace.

Nature's Palette of Emotions

The dawn breaks soft with golden light,
Each color dances, pure delight.
In forests deep, shades intertwine,
Nature's brushstrokes, so divine.

A canvas vast, with feelings bold,
In every petal, tales unfold.
Through seasons' shift, emotions sway,
In nature's art, I find my way.

The Sylvan Echo of My Being

In tangled woods where shadows fall,
I hear the whispers, nature's call.
Each rustling leaf, a story shared,
In sylvan realms, my soul laid bare.

Moments linger, soft and bright,
Reflections dance in the fading light.
The echoes of the past resound,
In every heartbeat, peace is found.

Spectrums of Seasonal Affection

Winter's chill brings thoughts so deep,
While spring awakens dreams from sleep.
Summer's laughter, joyous and free,
Filling the air with vibrant glee.

Autumn's whispers, warm and gold,
Embrace the tales of days untold.
In each season, love's embrace,
A spectrum rich, time can't erase.

A Symphony of Green and Gold

In fields where sunlight softly glows,
The dance of leaves, a whispered prose.
Golden grains in the gentle breeze,
Nature sings with perfect ease.

The emerald hills in twilight's embrace,
Each hue a note in this sacred space.
Rustling branches, a sweet refrain,
Harmony flows through the earth and grain.

Beneath the boughs, the shadows play,
A canvas brightening at the end of day.
In every creak, in every fold,
A symphony of green and gold.

With every step, the earth does sigh,
A melody under the vast, blue sky.
In whispers hushed, the world unfolds,
The timeless dance of nature holds.

Veils of Color in the Twilight

As dusk descends, the colors bloom,
Soft pastels weave through evening's loom.
Violet clouds drift slowly by,
Painting dreams across the sky.

Whispers of orange, hints of red,
A warm embrace where daylight fled.
The stars peek through, a twinkling tease,
In the silence, a gentle breeze.

Shadows stretch, while crickets play,
Nature hums, the end of day.
Veils of color, soft and bright,
Wrap the world in tender light.

Each moment lingers, a fleeting sigh,
As day bids farewell, the night draws nigh.
In twilight’s grasp, our hearts do soar,
Finding beauty forevermore.

Shadows Beneath the Canopy

Whispers of leaves dance with the breeze,
Soft echoes of time beneath ancient trees.
Shadows embrace where the sunlight glows,
Nature's secrets in hushed undertows.

Footsteps quietly tread on the ground,
In these dark corners, peace can be found.
The stories they tell, the dreams they hold,
In the tapestry woven, each thread turns to gold.

Nectar of Heartfelt Whispers

Sweet murmurs spill like honeyed wine,
Words wrapped in warmth, tender and fine.
Each secret shared, a blossom in bloom,
Filling the air with love's sweet perfume.

In the hush of night, passion ignites,
Moments entwined under silvery lights.
Hearts beat gently, their rhythm a song,
In the garden of whispers, where we belong.

Currents of Healing Soil

Beneath the earth, life stirs and grows,
Roots intertwine, as the wise earth knows.
Nurtured by rain, kissed by the sun,
In this sacred ground, all is one.

Hands in the dirt, we sow with care,
Dreams take flight on the warm spring air.
Healing begins in the fertile embrace,
Nature's bounty, a life we retrace.

Garden of Yearning Hues

Petals unfurl in a radiant spread,
Colors collide where the heart has led.
Each hue a whisper, each shade a song,
In the garden of yearning, we find where we belong.

Breezes carry the fragrance of desire,
Fires of passion that never tire.
In this vibrant realm, dreams softly fuse,
Crafting a mosaic of heartfelt hues.

Sheltered Glades of Connection

In the green embrace we find,
Soft whispers of a gentle breeze.
Sunlight dapples through the leaves,
Creating moments meant to seize.

Hearts entwined in quiet grace,
Where laughter dances in the air.
Beneath the branches' tender sway,
Love blossoms without a care.

Together in this tranquil space,
We share our stories, dreams, and fears.
Every glance, a silent vow,
In glades sheltered from the years.

Nature sings its sweetest song,
Reminding us we're not alone.
In these spaces, we belong,
A bond that feels like coming home.

Love's Blossoming Horizon

On the edge where skies ignite,
Colors blend in soft sunrise.
Every hue a whispered wish,
As love's light begins to rise.

With each petal's gentle fall,
Promises drift upon the breeze.
Tender moments intertwine,
Like branches swaying through the trees.

Hand in hand, we walk this path,
Toward a dawn that never fades.
Together crafting dreams anew,
On love's horizon, brightly laid.

In every heartbeat, every glance,
A world unfolds, rich and vast.
In this garden, hearts find peace,
A place where love will ever last.

Nature's Canvas of Resilience

Upon the canvas of the wild,
Colors dance with every season.
Life emerges fierce and bold,
Each moment holds its reason.

From shadows deep, the echoes rise,
Strength displayed in silent roots.
Through storms that threaten, still we bloom,
In nature's hands, our dreams take shoots.

The mountains stand, resolute and grand,
Against the trials they withstand.
In every crack and crevice found,
Life’s tenacity, a timeless brand.

So let us learn from earth’s embrace,
To weather change, to stand our ground.
In every struggle, we will trace,
The beauty in resilience found.

The Wyldwood's Heartfelt Expressions

Through twisted paths and winding trails,
Where echoes of the past reside.
The Wyldwood breathes in whispered tales,
Of love, and loss, where hearts confide.

Beneath the canopy of dreams,
Each leaf a memory, softly spun.
We dance among the moonlit beams,
With nature's song, our spirits run.

In the quiet, secrets bloom,
A tapestry of lives once lived.
Each rustling leaf, a destined room,
Where every heart can learn to forgive.

So in this wild and sacred space,
Let feelings flow, let worries fade.
In Wyldwood's arms, we find our place,
A sanctuary that won't trade.

Whispers of Blossoms

In the garden where silence sings,
Petals dance upon gentle springs.
Soft breezes carry fragrant dreams,
Whispers woven in sunlit beams.

Underneath the arching trees,
Nature hums in the softest breeze.
Colors brush the dawn's embrace,
Each bloom holds a sacred space.

Secret Seeds of Solitude

Beneath the soil, secrets lie,
Waiting for a gentle sigh.
Roots entangled in quiet grace,
Breathe life into this hidden place.

Moments linger in the shade,
Soft reflections never fade.
Whispers of the past take flight,
In shadows cool, beneath the light.

Petals of Hidden Dreams

In twilight's glow, the dreams unfold,
Stories whispered, softly told.
Petals drift like thoughts untamed,
Carried forth, yet all unnamed.

A canvas woven from the night,
Each hue a glimpse of lost delight.
With every breath, we chase the stream,
Searching forth for the hidden dream.

Tended by Moonlight

Under the gaze of silver skies,
Softly tread where the night flower lies.
Moonbeams sprinkle their gentle glow,
A tender light on dreams below.

Embrace the calm of night’s sweet breath,
Where shadows shroud the dance of death.
In luminescence, life will bloom,
Tended softly from the gloom.

Fragile Fragments of Joy

In morning light, laughter twirls,
A whisper through the dancing curls.
Moments slip like grains of sand,
Yet in our hearts, they make their stand.

A fleeting smile, a gentle touch,
These tiny gifts mean oh so much.
Though fleeting, they are worth the fight,
In shadows, they can spark the light.

We gather shards of bright delight,
In every glance, the heart takes flight.
With every tear, joy finds its way,
Fragile fragments bloom anew each day.

Roots of Resilience

Through storms and trials, we dig deep,
With silent strength, our secrets keep.
In fertile soil, our hopes reside,
Together strong, we won't divide.

Branches may sway, but will not break,
In unity, we weave and make.
From tiny seeds, great things can grow,
Roots of resilience in earth's warm glow.

Against the winds, we stand so tall,
In every challenge, we will not fall.
We rise like trees against the sky,
With roots entwined, we learn to fly.

Blooming in Stillness

In quietude, where thoughts can rest,
There lies a truth, in hearts expressed.
Petals unfurl in gentle graces,
In silence, beauty finds its places.

Deep breaths reveal the colors bright,
In stillness, we uncover light.
A bloom awakens, whispers sing,
In tranquil moments, life takes wing.

Each pause a chance, a sacred space,
Where dreams take shape, with tender grace.
In every heart, a garden grows,
Blooming in stillness, life bestows.

The Eternal Gardener

With hands of love, the gardener tends,
To every bud, where life begins.
In patient grace, the seasons turn,
Each garden speaks of what we learn.

Through sun and rain, the toil is bare,
In every thorn, a lesson rare.
The seeds of hope, in earth are sown,
In every heart, a truth is grown.

Nurturing dreams, with gentle care,
The gardener whispers to the air.
With gentle hands and watchful eyes,
The eternal gardener hears our sighs.

A Sanctuary of Colors

In the garden where blossoms sway,
Petals dance in the light of day.
Each hue whispers a gentle tune,
Colorful dreams beneath the moon.

Bees hum softly, their work divine,
In this haven, all hearts entwine.
Green leaves embrace the vibrant scenes,
Nature's palette fills in the greens.

With each breeze that rustles the trees,
A symphony flows as sweet as these.
Joy in the air, a fragrant delight,
In this sanctuary, pure and bright.

As twilight descends, shadows blend,
Colors fade, but love won't end.
Resting now, the day finds peace,
A tapestry of life, sweet release.

Songs of the Soil

Deep in the earth, where secrets lie,
The whispers of life, a soft sigh.
Seeds awaken to dawn's warm touch,
Their hopes reach high, they long for much.

Roots intertwine, a world unseen,
In the silence, a bond is keen.
Every grain holds a story old,
Yearning for light, their dreams unfold.

Beneath the surface, harmony plays,
As worms and bugs join in the frays.
The soil hums, a nourishing song,
A chorus of life, forever strong.

Harvests flourish in summer's glow,
From this embrace, the bounty grows.
Each fruit a testament, rich and full,
Songs of the soil, forever pull.

Where the Wildflowers Grow

In fields where wildflowers freely bloom,
Colors burst forth, dispelling gloom.
A tapestry woven by nature's hand,
Beauty unfurling across the land.

Bees and butterflies dance through the air,
In this wild place, life’s always fair.
Petals sway, kissed by the sun,
A celebration of life, never done.

With each breeze, the flowers sway,
Telling stories of a bright day.
Here in the wild, no fear, just grace,
Nature’s embrace, a sacred space.

As evening falls and colors fade,
Stars emerge, their dance displayed.
In dreams, we'll wander where they flow,
Into the heart of wildflowers aglow.

Nourished by Time

With each passing year, the trees grow wise,
Their branches stretch up to vast blue skies.
Stories linger in the rings revealed,
A testament to all they’ve healed.

The mountains stand tall, unmoved by change,
Their rugged peaks embrace the strange.
Time paints history on every stone,
A quiet strength in being alone.

Rivers carve paths through valleys deep,
Witnessing secrets that nature keeps.
Each ripple tells of journeys grand,
Nourished by time, the earth’s warm hand.

As the seasons turn in endless flow,
Life's rich tapestry continues to grow.
In every moment, there’s wisdom found,
Nourished by time, forever unbound.

The Blooming Within

In shadows deep where whispers dwell,
A seed of hope begins to swell.
Through cracks of doubt, it seeks the light,
With every breath, it claims its right.

The petals burst in vibrant hues,
A dance of colors, brave and true.
Each moment cherished, every sigh,
The bloom within prepares to fly.

Embracing the Thorns

Among the roses, thorns will rise,
A test of strength beneath the skies.
In every prick, a lesson found,
Resilience blooms upon the ground.

To hold the pain and beauty tight,
Is to embrace the dark and light.
With courage fierce, we'll face the storms,
In every heart, the spirit warms.

Sunlight's Gentle Caress

Morning breaks with softest light,
A golden kiss, a pure delight.
It nudges buds to stretch and sigh,
Inviting dreams to soar on high.

In beams of warmth, the world awakes,
A tender touch that kindness makes.
Each ray a promise, each glow a chance,
To revel in the sun's sweet dance.

Echoes of Roots and Rain

Beneath the surface, whispers flow,
The stories of the earth we know.
With every drop that falls, we find,
The strength of roots, the ties that bind.

In puddles formed, reflections gleam,
A chorus sung for those who dream.
The raindrops scatter, blessings shared,
In nature's arms, we are prepared.

Meadows of Silent Wishes

In fields where soft whispers lay,
Dreams dance with the light of day.
Petals drift on a gentle breeze,
Carrying secrets among the trees.

Silence speaks in the rustling grass,
Moments fade, and yet they pass.
Under the shade of a willow tall,
The heart listens to nature's call.

Here time stands still, quietly spun,
Among the meadows, we are one.
With each breath, a wish is made,
In this haven, fears do fade.

Golden sunlight kisses the dew,
Hopes arise, fresh and new.
Amongst the blooms, bright and free,
Wishes are sown for you and me.

Blooms Embracing the Sky

Colors burst where petals smile,
Reaching high, they stretch a while.
Softly swaying in radiant light,
Blooms embrace the sky, so bright.

In gardens rich, they sway and twirl,
Nature's wonders start to unfurl.
Every blossom, a tale to weave,
Whispering worlds we dare believe.

The fragrance dances, sweet and bold,
Stories of love and life unfold.
Among the vibrant hues that play,
Hope ignites in every ray.

When evening falls, they bow with grace,
Each petal holds a timeless space.
As stars above begin to wake,
The blooms will dream till dawn's first break.

Serenity Among the Greenery

In groves of quiet, peace is found,
Where leaves are gold and shades surround.
Here, the heart begins to pause,
Embracing nature's sacred cause.

Gentle whispers float on air,
Lifting worries, light and rare.
Every branch a tapestry,
Stitching moments into memory.

Nature hums a lullaby,
Beneath the vast and open sky.
With every breeze, the world feels light,
As shadows dance in soft twilight.

In this realm of lush, green dreams,
Life flows gently, or so it seems.
Each breath a step, serene and slow,
In this sanctuary, let love grow.

The Language of Colorful Roots

Roots entwined beneath the ground,
In silence, a connection's found.
Colors whisper through the earth,
Telling tales of life and birth.

Each hue a language, rich and wise,
Speaking softly, 'neath the skies.
Scarlet speaks of passion deep,
While azure lulls the soul to sleep.

In every shade, a story blooms,
In vibrant shades, life fills the rooms.
The dance of color, bright and bold,
Unveils the secrets we hold.

From roots to leaves, the message flows,
In every petal, love bestows.
Together, they weave a tapestry,
The language of roots, wild and free.

Memories Carved in Bark

In the forest's quiet hours,
Whispers echo through the trees.
Each carving tells a secret,
Of laughter, love, and gentle breeze.

Bark aged with time's embrace,
Stories etched in simple lines.
Nature’s canvas holds our past,
In the creases where life shines.

Knotty rings of circles spun,
Witness to the years elapsed.
Children's dreams and lovers' sighs,
All in wood, forever clasped.

As the seasons come and go,
Leaves fall softly to the ground.
Memories remain alive,
In each tree, a tale profound.

Garden Gateways to the Soul

Where petals stretch to greet the dawn,
Colors bloom in sweet array.
Gateways open, hearts respond,
In the garden, dreams at play.

Rustling leaves, a soothing hum,
Nature sings a gentle tune.
Footsteps follow winding paths,
Beneath the warmth of afternoon.

Each flower holds a secret wish,
Whispers shared with buzzing bees.
In their dance, we find our bliss,
Within their grace, we're truly free.

A refuge found in every green,
Solace in the vibrant hue.
Garden gateways always lead,
To the soul that yearns anew.

The Story of Each Bloom

In the morning light they grow,
Each petal holds a tale untold.
Colors bright and scents that flow,
Nature’s bounty, pure and bold.

From tiny seeds to mighty stems,
Each bloom a chapter of its own.
In every garden, whispers hem,
Life's beauty isn’t overgrown.

Sunlit hopes and rainy fears,
Seasons shape their fragrant grace.
Through laughter, love, and even tears,
The story finds its rightful place.

With every blossom, life renews,
Echoes of the past's sweet tune.
In every garden, there's a muse,
The story of each bloom, in bloom.

Luminescent Shadows of Passion

In the twilight's warm embrace,
Shadows dance with vibrant light.
Every whisper holds a trace,
Of passion's fire, burning bright.

Flickering dreams across the wall,
Hearts entwined beneath the stars.
In their glow, we feel the call,
Of love that knows no prison bars.

Each glance ignites a deeper spark,
In the silence, secrets sigh.
Luminescent shadows mark,
The moments that will never die.

With every heartbeat, embers flare,
Passion's rhythm, fierce and near.
In the night, we boldly dare,
To chase the dreams that draw us here.

Sowing Seeds of Hope

In the soil we plant our dreams,
Nurtured by the sun’s soft beams.
With each rain, they start to grow,
Whispers of a future glow.

Patience as the seasons pass,
Time will turn the grain to grass.
Every struggle brings the light,
Guiding us through darkest night.

Hands in dirt, the heart beats strong,
To the rhythm of nature's song.
With each seed, a promise sown,
A reminder, we're not alone.

Together, we will rise and thrive,
In the garden, hope's alive.
As the flowers bloom and sway,
Grateful for the light of day.

Flourishing in Solitude

In quiet corners, peace abides,
Where solitude's sweet charm resides.
Each moment, a gift to behold,
A sanctuary, calm and bold.

Beneath the trees, a gentle breeze,
Whispers secrets, hearts it frees.
In soft silence, thoughts take flight,
Guided by the stars at night.

Alone, yet not in emptiness,
In solitude, we find our rest.
As petals fall, a dance so light,
Flourishing in tender sight.

Here in stillness, we can grow,
Roots run deep, as rivers flow.
In the shadows, life will find,
The strength found in a tranquil mind.

Where Shadows Dance

In twilight's glow, shadows play,
Flirting with the night and day.
Shapes uncoil, and spirits rise,
A ballet spun beneath the skies.

Whispers echo, tales unfold,
Of dreams once lost, now brave and bold.
The moonlight casts a gentle veil,
While heartbeats weave an ancient tale.

In the stillness, time stands still,
As shadows stretch with quiet will.
They twirl and sway in mystic trance,
Inviting us to join the dance.

Together, we move as one,
Our fears dissolved in dusk's warm sun.
In this realm where dreams enhance,
Life reveals its sacred dance.

The Heart's Arboretum

In the grove of memory's tree,
Each leaf holds a story free.
Branches sway with secrets past,
In this haven, shadows cast.

Roots entwined, our journeys blend,
Love's embrace, a timeless friend.
Through seasons of joy and strife,
We're nurtured here, in this life.

In blossoms bright, hope reappears,
Amongst the laughter, and the tears.
The heart's arboretum thrives,
In every pulse, the spirit strives.

Through storms that bend and sway the boughs,
Here, we take our solemn vows.
In this garden, let us find,
The strength of love, forever kind.

The Enchanted Blossom

In a garden where dreams arise,
Petals whisper under the skies.
Colors dance in soft delight,
A wondrous bloom in morning light.

With dew-kissed grace, it sways so free,
Guarding secrets, a mystery.
Bees will hum their gentle tune,
As shadows play beneath the moon.

Each fragrance tells a tale unknown,
Of love and loss, of seeds once sown.
In twilight hours, enchantments weave,
A magic space where hearts believe.

Roots of Unexpressed Love

Beneath the surface, feelings grow,
Tangled whispers, soft and slow.
In silence, echoes softly bloom,
Lives entwined within the gloom.

Hearts concealed with tender might,
Shadows merge in the fading light.
Yearning sighs, a gaze that lingers,
Fingers brush like fleeting fingers.

Moments stolen, yet undone,
In the depths where dreams are spun.
With every pulse of life that flows,
Roots of love intertwine and grow.

Starlit Pathways of Emotion

Beneath the stars, our stories weave,
In twilight's grasp, we dare believe.
Each spark a wish, a dream in flight,
Guiding hearts through the endless night.

Whispers soft like a gentle breeze,
Moments captured among the trees.
Laughter dances on moonlit beams,
A tapestry of fragile dreams.

With every step, our spirits soar,
Along these trails, we seek for more.
In the hush of night, feelings rise,
Starlit pathways lead to the skies.

A Sanctuary of Solitude

In a quiet nook away from care,
Silence wraps me in its lair.
Whispers of winds in the trees,
Time unravels, life finds ease.

Beneath the branches, shadows play,
A moment held, softly it stays.
Within my heart, peace takes its throne,
In solitude, I find my own.

Thoughts like clouds drift far and wide,
In this haven, deep inside.
Embracing stillness, I shall find,
A sanctuary for my mind.

Echoes of Soft Breeze

Whispers dance through willow leaves,
A gentle touch, the heart believes.
Soft caresses in twilight's glow,
Nature's song, a sweet aglow.

The mountains sigh with every breeze,
Time stands still among the trees.
Ripples cradle silent dreams,
In the hush, the spirit gleans.

Flowers nod in rhythmic sway,
As dusk begins to end the day.
Stars awaken, softly gleam,
In the night, we dare to dream.

Echoes linger, softly bound,
In the silence, love is found.
Each whisper leads to paths unknown,
In this solace, we are home.

Heartstrings in Nature's Embrace

In the meadow, wild hearts roam,
Nature cradles them like home.
Petals blush beneath the sun,
Threads of love, they're gently spun.

The streams reflect our deepest song,
In the wild, where hearts belong.
Beneath the boughs, we find our peace,
In moments fleeting, joys increase.

Whispers float on zephyr's breath,
Life and love entwined in death.
Each rustling leaf has tales to share,
Of heartstrings held with tender care.

In twilight's glow, our dreams unite,
Underneath the starry night.
Nature's pulse, a heartbeat bold,
In her arms, our stories told.

Ferns of Unexpressed Yearnings

In shadows deep, the ferns reside,
Guarding dreams we dare not hide.
Their fronds unfurl like whispered sighs,
In silent pleas beneath the skies.

Underneath the emerald shade,
Unseen wishes softly laid.
Each curve a secret, deeply grown,
In their grace, our hearts have sown.

Moistened earth embraces night,
While stars weave patterns, pure and bright.
In the stillness, silence speaks,
Of tender hope that softly peaks.

From ancient roots, our stories sprout,
In ferns of longing, dreams clout.
Each heartbeat syncs with nature's flow,
In quiet realms, our passions grow.

Fables of Flora and Emotion

Once in glades where shadows play,
Flora weaves her tales each day.
With petals bright and scents so sweet,
In her stories, our hearts meet.

Leaves tell whispers of the past,
Each moment, a spell cast.
Through blossoms bold, emotions soar,
In nature's hands, we’re evermore.

The brook hums ancient melodies,
While breezes carry sacred keys.
Touched by sunlight’s warm embrace,
In every bloom, love finds its place.

Fables flourish in diverse hues,
With every glance, a world renewed.
In this garden of timeless grace,
We find ourselves in nature's space.

Scented Memories Beneath the Stars

Whispers of night dance on the breeze,
Carrying scents of memories past,
Under a sky of twinkling light,
We held onto dreams that would not last.

The moonlight paints our shadows long,
Silhouettes of laughter, hopes, and fears,
In this enchanted realm, we belong,
As we gather all the fleeting years.

Fragrant blooms entwine our thoughts,
Each petal echoes stories untold,
In the garden of hearts, we sought,
A tapestry of moments to hold.

Beneath the stars, we pause and sigh,
Each fragrance a bridge to yesterday,
With every breath, we learn to fly,
In scented memories, we find our way.

The Whimsy of Wildflowers

Amidst the green, wildflowers sway,
A riotous burst of color and cheer,
They dance with glee in bright array,
Spreading joy as springtime draws near.

Petals giggle in the soft sunlight,
While bees hum sweet notes in the air,
Each bloom a treasure, pure delight,
Whispering secrets we long to share.

In meadows wide, the laughter sings,
As nature's palette strokes the ground,
A canvas woven with gentle strings,
In simple beauty, happiness found.

Let us wander where the wild things grow,
In the whims of wildflowers' embrace,
For in their charm, our spirits flow,
Awakening joy in every space.

Thorns of Past Regret

In a garden where shadows creep,
Thorns entwined with memories old,
Each prick a reminder, a wound to keep,
The tales of dreams that turned to gold.

Echoes linger in the evening air,
Of choices made and paths not taken,
A heavy heart, lost in despair,
The seeds of hope, so often shaken.

Yet through the thorns, a rose can bloom,
Resilience found in sorrow's gaze,
For every moment steeped in gloom,
Can lead to brighter, hopeful days.

So let us cherish what we’ve learned,
From the thorns and scars that time bestows,
In the garden of life, the heart is turned,
To find the beauty that each story shows.

Grace Among the Daisies

Among the daisies, pure and bright,
Life unfolds in soft embrace,
With gentle grace and golden light,
Each petal tells a tale of space.

The sun gifts warmth to every bloom,
As whispers fuse with morning dew,
In fields where thoughts are free to loom,
We find ourselves, refreshed and new.

In simplicity, the heart will soar,
With every glance, a moment saved,
Among the daisies, we explore,
The beauty found in love's soft wave.

So let us wander, hand in hand,
With grace that only nature brings,
In the dance of daisies, we will stand,
And celebrate what living means.

Fragrant Paths of Introspection

Along the winding lane I tread,
Petals whisper secrets, softly spread.
The air is filled with memories sweet,
In quiet corners, where heartbeats meet.

Beneath the arching trees I pause,
Nature holds me in gentle laws.
Each breath a journey, each step a rhyme,
I lose myself in this sacred time.

Footprints fade on soft earth's skin,
With every heartbeat, new dreams begin.
A fragrant path leads deep within,
Where light and shadow softly spin.

Turning leaves and breezes sigh,
I muse on moments, as they fly.
In fragrant paths of introspection,
I find my heart’s true direction.

Tides of Blossom and Memory

In gardens bright where blossoms sway,
Memories linger, come what may.
Each bud unfurls, a tale retold,
In hues of blush and marigold.

The gentle breeze brings whispers near,
Of laughter shared and joyful cheer.
With every petal that takes flight,
A story dances, pure delight.

Waves of color wash ashore,
As time unfolds, forevermore.
In tides of blossom, hearts entwine,
With fragrant dreams and love's design.

As dusk descends, the stars ignite,
Illuminating the cherished night.
In every bloom, a piece of me,
In tides of memory, I am free.

Resonance of Lush Serenity

In emerald glades where silence reigns,
A tranquil heart sheds all its chains.
Each rustling leaf, a soothing song,
A symphony where I belong.

Cool waters flow, reflecting skies,
Nature's whispers softly rise.
With every breath, I feel alive,
In this lush peace, my spirit thrives.

The melody of dusk descends,
As twilight wraps and daylight bends.
Beneath the stars, all worries cease,
In resonance, I find my peace.

Here time stands still, the world suspends,
In harmony where beauty blends.
In lush serenity, my soul is free,
With nature's love, I simply be.

Chasing Fluttering Butterflies

In fields where wildflowers bloom so bright,
I chase the dreams that take to flight.
Butterflies dance on the whims of air,
Each flutter whispers, a wish laid bare.

Through golden rays and shadows cast,
I run with laughter, forgetting the past.
Each vibrant color, a fleeting glance,
Inviting me to join the dance.

With grace they weave through sunlit seams,
A tapestry woven from childhood dreams.
In their wake, I find joy untold,
Chasing wonders, both timid and bold.

As evening falls and stars appear,
I hold close the magic, so near.
In chasing butterflies, I see,
A part of the dream lives wild and free.

Delicate Traces of Affection

In whispers soft, our hearts align,
Like shadows cast on dusk's design.
Each gentle touch, a sweet refrain,
A tapestry of joy and pain.

In secret glances, love ignites,
As blooming stars fill lonely nights.
With every sigh, we weave a thread,
Of quiet dreams, where hopes are fed.

Through fleeting moments, bonds are spun,
A dance of souls, two hearts as one.
So fragile yet, this cherished grace,
We trace with care, each warm embrace.

As time unfolds, the echoes stay,
In delicate traces, come what may.
Our love's soft imprint, always there,
In every breath, a whispered prayer.

Vines of Untold Stories

Amidst the leaves, the secrets grow,
In tangled roots, the stories flow.
Each vine a path, a tale to share,
Of whispered winds and fragrant air.

With every twist, a memory clings,
Of laughter's light and heart's soft wings.
Through shadows deep, the truth will strive,
In silent whispers, we stay alive.

In twilight's blush, the past unwinds,
Revealing the love that fate entwines.
The vines of time, both brave and bold,
Conceal within, their tales untold.

And as we walk, in nature's fold,
We'll harvest dreams, both new and old.
With open hearts, we'll tend the vine,
And press our spirits into the twine.

Aromas of Lingering Hope

In morning's light, a fragrance plays,
Of sunlit dreams and golden rays.
Each breath we take, a soft embrace,
Of lingering hope in sacred space.

Through whispered winds, the scents arrive,
Reminding us that we survive.
With every bloom, a chance to rise,
To find the beauty in the skies.

The petals whisper tales of strife,
Yet fragrance thrives, the pulse of life.
In tender moments, dreams ignite,
As warmth enfolds the chill of night.

With open arms, we greet each day,
In aromas bright, our fears allay.
So breathe in deep, let sweetness flow,
For in our hearts, there’s always hope.

The Sylvan Spectrum of Feelings

In quiet woods, where shadows play,
The mind retreats; the heart's at bay.
Each rustling leaf, a secret shared,
In sylvan halls, all burdens bared.

With every step on nature's floor,
We find the peace we're longing for.
In vibrant hues, the world aligns,
A spectrum rich, where love entwines.

The branches weave, a canopy,
Of whispered thoughts, serene and free.
Each color speaks of joy and pain,
In nature’s realm, no loss in vain.

Through every path, each winding bend,
We gather strength, to make amends.
So let us wander, hand in hand,
In sylvan dreams, together stand.

Echoing in the Meadow's Whisper

In the meadow, soft winds play,
Echoes dance in sun's warm ray.
Whispers weave through blades of green,
Nature's song, a tranquil scene.

Shadows stretch where daisies bloom,
Each petal holds the scent of gloom.
Yet laughter lingers in the air,
In this quiet, I feel bare.

Clouds drift slowly, dreams in flight,
Fleeting moments, pure delight.
The whisper calls, I must be still,
In the meadow, time does thrill.

Here I find my heart's true voice,
In the breeze, I make my choice.
To follow where the whispers lead,
Among the blooms, my soul is freed.

Kaleidoscope of Heartfelt Hues

Colors burst in wild embrace,
A canvas bright, a sacred space.
Each shade tells a story bold,
Of warmth and love, a joy to hold.

Reds of passion, blues of dreams,
Life unfolds in vibrant streams.
Greens of hope and yellows bright,
Each hue a piece of pure delight.

As twilight casts its golden glow,
The palette shifts, emotions flow.
In this kaleidoscope, we sway,
Finding magic in the day.

Together, we paint the skies,
Underneath the endless ties.
In heartfelt hues, we exist,
Each moment cherished, not dismissed.

Soft Serenades Among the Blooms

In gardens lush, the blossoms sway,
Soft serenades greet the day.
Petals flutter with gentle grace,
Nature's choir sets the pace.

Honeybees hum a sweet refrain,
Dancing lightly, free of chain.
Lilies nod, while roses blush,
In this haven, hearts can hush.

The fragrance wraps like a warm embrace,
Each bloom a memory, time, and place.
Among the blooms, I feel alive,
In this symphony, I thrive.

Beneath the sky, our spirits bound,
In soft serenades, love is found.
Together we sing, hearts in tune,
Among the blooms, beneath the moon.

Each Leaf a Silent Confession

Each leaf rustles in the breeze,
A whisper shared among the trees.
Secrets linger in their veins,
Silent truths, love's soft refrains.

Golden hues in autumn's light,
Nature's canvas, pure delight.
With each flutter, tales unfold,
Of laughter, sorrow, love untold.

And when the winter's chill descends,
Bare branches twist, the silence blends.
Yet hope springs forth with spring's embrace,
New leaves awaken, filling space.

In every season, lessons gleaned,
Nature's stories, intertwined and deemed.
Each leaf, a whisper from above,
A testament to life and love.

Dreams Blooming in Silence

In the hush of night’s embrace,
Soft whispers weave through space.
Stars blink slowly, dreams take flight,
Cradled in the arms of night.

Petals fall without a sound,
In the garden, peace is found.
Fragrant hopes begin to rise,
Underneath the silent skies.

Gentle thoughts like shadows play,
Guiding hearts along the way.
In the stillness, visions gleam,
Lost within a waking dream.

Embrace the calm, let it be,
In the silence, we are free.
Through the quiet, love will bloom,
Filling every hidden room.

Moonlit Roses of Reflection

Beneath the glow of silver light,
Roses whisper in the night.
Petals glisten, shadowed glow,
Secrets of the heart they show.

Each bloom tells a story rare,
Of love and loss, a tender care.
Moonbeams dance on velvet leaves,
In their presence, time deceives.

Reflections cast in tranquil hues,
Breathe the essence of our muse.
In the garden, silence sings,
Carrying the peace it brings.

In the stillness, dreams take flight,
Wrapped in the calm of night.
Moonlit roses, soft and bright,
Guide the heart towards the light.

Waters of Tranquil Inspiration

Ripples form on gentle streams,
Whispers drift like feathered dreams.
A canvas painted in the flow,
Carrying secrets that we know.

Silver surfaces calm the mind,
In their depths, solace we find.
Each drop sings a soothing song,
Where the heart can feel it belong.

Beneath the surface, shadows play,
Echoes of the words we say.
Flowing softly, gracefully,
Water's dance, a symphony.

In the quiet, spirits rise,
Reflecting back the endless skies.
Waters deep of pure delight,
Inspiration's softest light.

The Essence of Petal Poetry

In the bloom of morning's grace,
Petals whisper, time and space.
Colors brush across the day,
In their softness, words will play.

Nature's verse, a silent speak,
In every fold, the heart will sneak.
As fragrance mingles with the air,
Petal poetry, beyond compare.

Dewdrops glisten where they lie,
Beneath the vast and endless sky.
Each petal tells a tale so true,
Of the love that once we knew.

In the garden, time stands still,
Capturing dreams with gentle will.
The essence of our hopes now flows,
In the poetry of petals' throes.

Threads of Nature's Tapestry

In the weave of green and gold,
Life's stories gently unfold.
Leaves like whispers dance in air,
A tapestry beyond compare.

From the roots that tangle deep,
To the branches where secrets sleep.
Every thread holds light and shade,
Nature’s beauty, art portrayed.

Colors collide in vibrant embrace,
A vibrant world, a sacred space.
Each petal sings with morning dew,
A testament of life anew.

Whispers of the Secret Grove

In shadows where the sunlight fades,
Mysteries of the forest wade.
Ancient trees with stories old,
Guard the secrets they behold.

Softly spoken, the breeze does hum,
Inviting all to come, to come.
Every rustle, every sigh,
Echoes of the days gone by.

Amidst the ferns, a path appears,
Leading us to calm, not fears.
The grove whispers, softly clear,
Embracing all who wander near.

Blossoms of the Inner Sanctuary

In the heart where silence blooms,
Light dances in the quiet rooms.
Petals unfold like dreams at night,
In this peace, the soul takes flight.

Fragrance lingers in the air,
Easing burdens, lightening care.
Softly colors blend and sway,
Guiding thoughts that drift away.

Within each bud, a story waits,
Of hope, of love, and opened gates.
In this realm, the heart can heal,
Embraced by beauty, pure and real.

Echoes of the Soul's Oasis

In stillness where reflections play,
The soul finds rest at end of day.
Ripples shimmer on the lake,
Each echo whispers, peace awake.

Under stars that softly gleam,
We dive deep into the dream.
Moments linger, sweet and bright,
In this sanctuary of light.

Silhouettes of dusk take form,
Whispers of the heart, the norm.
Beneath the moon's gentle glow,
Each breath reveals what we can sow.

Curls of Lavender and Time

In fields where lavender sways,
Soft whispers carry the haze.
Time curls gently like the breeze,
A dance of memories with ease.

Each petal holds a secret song,
In twilight's glow, we drift along.
The lavender sighs, a sweet retreat,
Embracing moments, bittersweet.

The clock ticks softly, never loud,
In the stillness, we are proud.
With every hue, the sky extends,
A tapestry where day transcends.

So let us wander, hand in hand,
Through curls of lavender, we stand.
Time flows like rivers, deep and wide,
In fragrant dreams, we shall abide.

Sunsets Through the Petal Veil

Golden rays on petals lie,
As day whispers a soft goodbye.
The sky blushes in fading light,
A canvas painting the night.

Through blooms of color, we perceive,
The beauty in what we believe.
Soft petals catch the warmth's embrace,
In this twilight, we find our place.

Sunset drapes a silken shawl,
Each shadow weaves a gentle call.
Nature’s palette colors the air,
A moment though fleeting, so rare.

As stars peek through the evening shade,
We linger still in the cascade.
Forever, sunsets guide our way,
Through the petal veil, we shall stay.

The Fruitfulness of Emotion

Emotions bloom like fruit in spring,
Colorful hearts begin to sing.
Joy, sorrow, love intertwined,
A tapestry of the human mind.

With every tear and every laugh,
We carve our stories, each a path.
The sweetness savored, bitter too,
In every bite, we start anew.

Like gardens rich with life and grace,
The fruitfulness we must embrace.
With open palms, we gather round,
In every heartbeat, life is found.

So let us taste the varied hues,
Of feelings deep, both old and new.
In every fruit, a tale to share,
The goodness of emotion laid bare.

Glistening Pathways of Joy

In morning's light, the dew bestows,
A shimmer on the earth that flows.
Each pathway glistens, calling bright,
With joy that dances in the light.

Through forests green and skies of blue,
We wander pathways, tried and true.
With laughter echoing through the trees,
The heart finds solace in the breeze.

Glistening highways stretch ahead,
Where dreams of wonder gently tread.
Each step unveils a vibrant view,
A world alive with hope anew.

So let us walk this joyful trail,
With every heartbeat, we shall sail.
In glistening moments, find our place,
And celebrate the joy we grace.

Petals of Unseen Dreams

In twilight's glow, the shadows sigh,
Whispers of hopes that learn to fly.
Each petal drops with silent grace,
Carrying dreams we dare not face.

Beneath the stars, a secret stream,
Where night blooms softly, weaving dream.
With every breath, the silence breaks,
Hearts tune to what the darkness makes.

In gardens far from common sight,
The moonlit paths unveil the night.
Each step reveals a hidden fate,
Petals dance dream's sacred state.

So let us wander, spirits free,
Among the paths of mystery.
For in the stillness, hope redeems,
The tender touch of unseen dreams.

The Hidden Orchard's Serenade

In a grove where secrets lie,
Whispers of the past drift by.
Orchard blooms with sweet perfume,
Harmony in nature's room.

Softly strummed on branches low,
Melodies of time bestow.
Each note, a tale of days gone,
Echoes in the early dawn.

Underneath the dappled shade,
Quiet footsteps gently made.
Nature’s song, both rich and pure,
In this haven, hearts endure.

So linger ‘neath this leafy dome,
Where the wild things call you home.
With every sigh, the fruits declare,
A serenade beyond compare.

Tapestry of Forgotten Fragrance

In woven threads of yesteryears,
Lies a scent that stirs old fears.
Petals crushed beneath the weight,
Remind us of our fragile fate.

Through time’s embrace, the echoes call,
Faint whispers rise and softly fall.
Each fragrance holds a story dear,
Of love and loss, of joy and fear.

The tapestry, a vivid hue,
Holds memories in every view.
Intertwined in life's design,
We find the paths by fate's align.

So breathe in deep the faded air,
Let the past with present share.
For in the scents that linger still,
Lies the strength of nature’s will.

Secrets Among the Leaves

Beneath the canopy so green,
Whispers float, though seldom seen.
Each leaf a tale, each rustle clear,
Nature's voice, both calm and near.

In shadows cast by light’s soft dance,
Lies a world that dares to prance.
Tiny creatures scurry by,
Lost in dreams beneath the sky.

The wind carries a gentle sigh,
Secrets held where echoes lie.
With every breeze, a story told,
Of timeless truths and yesterdays old.

So pause awhile, and take it in,
The wisdom found where leaves begin.
For in this place of tranquil ease,
Lies the heart of nature's keys.

A Haven of Quietude

In the shade where soft winds sigh,
Whispers of peace gently pass by.
A sanctuary under the trees,
Where all worries drift off with ease.

Sunlight dapples on the ground,
In stillness, a solace found.
Moments stretch; time stands still,
A heart at rest, a quiet thrill.

Birdsong weaves through emerald space,
Nature's rhythm, a warm embrace.
Here the soul can pause and breathe,
In tranquil corners, we believe.

The world fades, as shadows blend,
In a haven where calm transcends.
A perfect balm for weary eyes,
In this quietude, the spirit flies.

The Language of Leaves

Each leaf tells stories of the past,
In rustling whispers, echoes cast.
With colors bright, they dance in light,
Their secrets shared, a gentle sight.

In autumn's glow, they fall like dreams,
Carried by winds, in silver streams.
A tapestry woven with nature's grace,
In each soft fold, a hidden place.

The green of spring, the gold of fall,
In every season, they recount all.
A dialogue between earth and sky,
In the language of leaves, we learn to fly.

Stoic and wise, they stand tall,
Reflecting the life's rise and fall.
In every shimmer, the past believed,
A speaking world, forever conceived.

Dew-Kissed Reflections

Morning light through window panes,
Catching glimmers on soft plains.
Each droplet weaves a crystal spell,
In their beauty, silence dwells.

Like tiny mirrors, they hold the morn,
Where dreams awaken, new hopes are born.
Glistening pearls on blades of grass,
Moments quicken and gently pass.

The world reflected, calm and clear,
In these treasures, all is near.
Nature's touch, a soft caress,
In dew-kissed wonders, we find our rest.

As shadows stretch and day unfolds,
Each spark of light a story holds.
In every droplet, life takes flight,
Awakening joy in morning light.

When Ferns Take Flight

In quiet woods, where whispers soar,
Ferns stretch upward, wanting more.
With fronds unfurled, they seek the sky,
An earthy dance, a soft goodbye.

They sway with grace, in rhythms sweet,
A gentle pulse beneath our feet.
In shades of green, they rise and bend,
As if the ground could thus transcend.

When breezes come, they twist and twirl,
A ballet found in nature's whirl.
Each leaf a feather, light, and free,
Ferns take flight in harmony.

In emerald bosks, the worlds collide,
Where ferns unfold with gentle pride.
An ancient song, a tender sight,
In nature's arms, we feel their flight.

The Symphony of Sprouts

In the morning light they rise,
Tiny green whispers of the earth.
Dancing gently with the breeze,
They hum a song of rebirth.

Roots entwined beneath the soil,
Reaching for the warmth above.
A symphony of growth unfolds,
Nurtured by the sun's pure love.

Each leaf a note within the choir,
Swaying softly to the tune.
Nature's orchestra inspired,
Beneath the watchful moon.

In this concert, life prevails,
A harmony of joy and peace.
The symphony of sprouts, we hear,
A promise of the sweet release.

Cradled in Nature's Embrace

Underneath the ancient trees,
A shelter soft and safe, we find.
Whispers of the gentle breeze,
Soothes the weary heart and mind.

Petals fall like tender dreams,
Kissed by sunlight, warm and bright.
In this sacred space, it seems,
All worries fade with day to night.

Cascading streams of laughter flow,
Among the moss and fragrant trails.
Each moment here, a gentle glow,
Where nature's love forever prevails.

Cradled close, we breathe in deep,
The essence woven through each tree.
In nature's arms, our spirits leap,
Forever held, forever free.

Harvesting Serenity

In the fields of golden grain,
We gather peace beneath the sky.
Each moment free from worldly pain,
As gentle breezes whisper by.

Hands that toil with love and care,
Pulling forth the fruits of grace.
In the quiet, we become aware,
Of beauty found in each embrace.

Days unfold with each new dawn,
Filling baskets with sweet joy.
With open hearts, we move along,
Harvesting what life can deploy.

Serenity, our greatest prize,
We cherish in each simple deed.
As the sun sinks and time flies,
We find abundance in our need.

The Garden of Yearning

In shadows cast by quiet trees,
Desires bloom like flowers rare.
Each petal holds a whispered plea,
In the stillness of the air.

Tendrils stretch towards the light,
Reaching for what lies ahead.
In this garden, dreams take flight,
As hopes are nurtured, gently fed.

Every seed, a wish to grow,
Watered by the tears we shed.
In the depths of heart's echo,
Yearning blossoms, courage bred.

The garden sings of what’s to come,
In every root, a story stays.
With patience, find where we’re from,
In yearning's grace, the spirit sways.

Milton Keynes UK
Ingram Content Group UK Ltd.
UKHW021951151124
451186UK00007B/191

9 789916 906583